D1480458

Volcano Escape!

Kathleen Weidner Zoehfeld

RANDOM HOUSE 🏠 NEW YORK

p. i © Greg Vaughn/Alamy Stock Photo; p. 8 © USGS; p. 9 © Sailorr/Shutterstock; p. 10 © Wead/Shutterstock; p. 11 © servickuz/Shutterstock; p. 12 © S-F/Shutterstock; p. 15 © BlueRingMedia/Shutterstock; p. 16 © honglouwawa/Shutterstock; p. 17 © Tyler Boyes/Shutterstock; p. 18–19 © www.sandatlas.org/Shutterstock; p. 20 © Brian Overcast/Alamy Stock Photo; p. 21 © Jesús Eloy Ramos Lara/Dreamstime; p. 22 © USGS; p. 25 © Vitoriano Junior/Shutterstock; p. 26 © Pierre Leclerc/Shutterstock; p. 28–29 © Greg Vaughn/Alamy Stock Photo; p. 30 © USGS; p. 31 © Daxiao Productions/Shutterstock; p. 32 © Stocktrek Images, Inc./Alamy Stock Photo; p. 33 © N.Minton/Shutterstock; p. 34 © neelsky/Shutterstock; p. 35 © Alexey Kamenskiy/Shutterstock; p. 36 © Marisa Estivill/Shutterstock; p. 37 (top) © Sekar B/Shutterstock; p. 37 (bottom) © bierchen/Shutterstock; p. 38 © Krishna.Wu/Shutterstock; p. 39 © Nina B/Shutterstock; p. 40 © Jim West/Alamy Stock Photo; p. 41 © USGS; p. 42 © robertharding/Alamy Stock Photo; p. 44 © Matyas Rehak/Shutterstock; p. 45 © Reuters/CORBIS; p. 47 © Rat007/Shutterstock; p. 48 © ZinaidaSopina/Shutterstock; p. 49 © Zach Holmes/Alamy Stock Photo; p. 51 © National Geographic Creative/Alamy Stock Photo; p. 52 © USGS; p. 53 © USGS; p. 55 © Boris Sosnovyy/Shutterstock; p. 56 (top) © www.sandatlas.org/Shutterstock; p. 56 (bottom) Tom Grundy/Shutterstock; p. 57 © www.sandatlas.org/Shutterstock; p. 58 © Leene/Shutterstock; p. 59 (top left) © ronnybas/Shutterstock; p. 59 (top right) © Bill Perry/Shutterstock; p. 59 (bottom) © ermess/Shutterstock; p. 60 © Vladislav Gajic/Shutterstock; p. 61 (granite) © Gyvafoto/Shutterstock; p. 61 (limestone) © michal812/Shutterstock; p. 61 (sandstone) © Alexlukin/Shutterstock; p. 61 (basalt, gneiss, marble, phyllite, quartzite, schist, slate) © Tyler Boyes/Shutterstock; p. 63 © godrick/Shutterstock; p. 64–65 (bottom), 65 (top), 66 (top), 66 (bottom), 68 courtesy of NASA; p. 69 (top) © Art Directors & TRIP/Alamy Stock Photo; p. 69 (bottom) courtesy of NASA/JPL-Caltech

Cover photograph copyright © by Fotos593/Shutterstock

Published in the United States by Random House Children's Books, a division of Penguin Random House LLC, New York.

Random House and the colophon are registered trademarks of Penguin Random House LLC.

Visit us on the Web! randomhousekids.com

Educators and librarians, for a variety of teaching tools, visit us at RHTeachersLibrarians.com

Library of Congress Cataloging-in-Publication Data
Zoehfeld, Kathleen Weidner, author.
School of dragons : volcano escape! / Kathleen Weidner Zoehfeld.
p. cm. — (School of dragons)
Audience: Ages 7–10.
Audience: Grades 2 to 5.
ISBN 978-1-101-93337-4 (trade) — ISBN 978-1-101-93338-1 (lib. bdg.) — ISBN 978-1-101-93339-8 (ebook)
1. Volcanoes—Juvenile literature. I. Title. II. Title: Volcano escape!
QE521.3.Z64 2016 551.21—dc23 2015030597

Printed in the United States of America 10 9 8 7 6 5 4 3 2 1

Contents

Note to Readers

What do dragons have to do with real-life science and history?
More than you might think!

For thousands of years, cultures all over the world have told stories about dragons, just as they told fanciful tales about unicorns, fairies, mermaids, ogres, and other mythical creatures. People made up these and other legends for many reasons: to explain the natural world, to give their lives deeper meaning, sometimes even just for fun! Stories passed down from generation to generation began to change over time. In many cases, fact (what's true) and fiction (what's made up) blended together to create a rich legacy of storytelling.

So even though you don't see them flying overhead, dragons are all around us! They are a part of our history and culture, bridging the gap between the past and the present — what's real and what's born of our limitless imaginations. This makes the *DreamWorks Dragons* Dragon Riders ideal candidates to teach us about our world!

Think of the School of Dragons series as your treasure map to a land of fascinating facts about science, history, mythology, culture, innovation, and more! You can read the books cover to cover or skip around to sections that most interest you. There's no right or wrong way when it comes to learning.

And that's not all! When you're done reading the books, you can go online to schoolofdragons.com to play the interactive School of Dragons video games from JumpStart. There's no end to what you can discover. Be sure to check out the inside back cover of this book for a special game code that will allow you access to super-secret adventures!

All ready? Hold on tight, dragon trainers! Here we go . . .

Meet the Characters

Astrid

Hiccup

Snotlout

Stoick the Vast

Fishlegs

Gobber

Ruffnut & Tuffnut

Meet the Dragons

Toothless
Species: Night Fury

Barf & Belch
Species: Hideous Zippleback

Hookfang
Species: Monstrous Nightmare

Meatlug
Species: Gronckle

Stormfly
Species: Deadly Nadder

Understanding Volcanoes

Most people go through their whole lives without expecting a nearby mountain to explode. They don't worry about avalanches of fiery hot rock and ash. They don't wonder if their houses and schools will be buried. . . .

But in some places, the ground shakes and the mountains roar! Places where super-hot rock comes up from deep inside the Earth are called **volcanoes.** When a volcano erupts, tons of hot rock and ash come crashing down. They destroy everything in their path.

Volcanoes are even more powerful than dragons!

Mount Vesuvius in Italy

People who live near volcanoes sometimes get scared. Why do mountains explode? What can people do to keep safe?

Since ancient times, people have tried to understand volcanoes. The Romans had many myths that helped them make sense of the world around them. The word *volcano* comes from one of these stories. In Roman mythology, Vulcan was the god of fire. Vulcan was said to live under a very violent volcano named Mount Etna.

On August 24, 79 CE, something strange was going on with the Roman mountain **Vesuvius.** The ground around it was shaking, but this was nothing new. There were lots of earthquakes in this area. But this time, the mountain was rumbling, and a very odd cloud was forming over

Mount Vesuvius and ruins from Pompeii, Italy

the mountain's peak. The cloud was narrow at the bottom, like a tree trunk, but it rose up high and spread out wide.

A leader in the Roman navy, Pliny the Elder, came out of his house to take a look. He was one of the world's **naturalists,** which

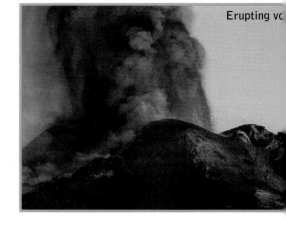

Erupting vc

means he studied the natural world all around him. Pliny was not impressed by stories of gods under mountains. He wanted to know the truth. He ordered his men to get the boats ready. They were going to row as close to the mountain as possible.

Sometimes solving problems takes brains and brawn.

Meanwhile, the ground near Vesuvius began to shake violently. Nearby towns could hear a booming worse than thunder. They were showered with rock and ash. The terrible sounds got louder by the minute. The volcanic cloud grew so thick it blotted out the sun. The day became as dark as night. Lightning struck the mountaintop. Ash and rock rained down from above.

Volcanic eruptions remind me of angry dragons!

This volcanic rock is pumice. It is light and airy and can even float in water. If it's raining pumice, you could be in trouble—it means a volcano has exploded!

Pliny took notes during the eruption. When it was over, Pliny's nephew, Pliny the Younger, put together his uncle's notes and his own observations. He shared his work with a friend who was an historian so that others could learn about the volcano, too. His description of the eruption was so precise that explosive eruptions like this are now known as **Plinian eruptions.**

Pompeii was a town near Vesuvius in 79 CE. During the eruption, roofs were pounded by falling **pumice!** A deep layer of ash filled the streets, blocking doors and windows. People who stayed indoors were trapped. Outside, people

Towns like Pompeii were buried right up over the tallest rooftops. Today you can visit Pompeii and see what happened for yourself!

tied pillows on their heads to protect themselves from the falling rocks. They tried to run to safety through the chest-deep ash. They held cloths over their faces to keep from choking on the dust and smoke. But there was no escaping their fate.

What could the people in these towns have done differently? First, they should have left the area as soon as they heard explosions and saw the strange cloud. They may have escaped in time.

We have come a long way since Pliny the Younger's first account of volcanoes. Scientists continue to study volcanoes, hoping to understand them better and find ways to keep people safe when they do erupt.

We need to find out what's going on in our Hatchery!

Inside the Earth

Since ancient times, humans have wondered where volcanic ash and melted rock come from. For many years, **geologists**—scientists who study the Earth—thought that the Earth had a huge fiery center and that melted rock came up through underground tunnels. It was hard to be sure. Geologists could not see inside the Earth!

Then, in the 1800s, scientists invented a tool called a **seismometer.** When an earthquake strikes or a volcano erupts, the ground moves and shakes. Seismometers measure and record movements deep inside the Earth. Geologists set up seismometers all around the world. This gave them

Seismometer

- frame
- wire
- weight
- rotating drum
- vibrations
- base

information about what Earth is like beneath the surface.

Today, we know that there are no volcanic tunnels underground. We also know that Earth does not have a fiery center (although it is very hot there!).

Sometimes we feel the ground shake near the Hatchery!

Earth diagram

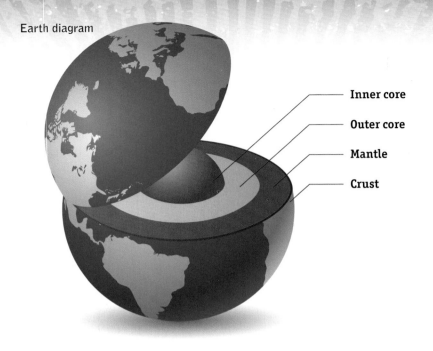

Inner core

Outer core

Mantle

Crust

Earth is made up of several layers. At the center is the **inner core.** The inner core is a solid ball made up of two metals: iron and nickel. The temperature in this layer is close to 9,000 degrees Fahrenheit (5,000 degrees Celsius). That's as hot as the surface of the sun! That much heat should melt the inner core, but there is so much pressure that it stays solid.

Around the inner core, there is an **outer core** of hot liquid metal. Around the outer core is a thick layer of super-hot rock: the **mantle.**

The outermost layer of Earth is called the **crust.** This is the layer we live on. Compared to the size of Earth's other layers, the crust is very thin. Under the oceans, the crust is around four miles (seven kilometers) thick. On land, it can be more than thirty-seven miles (sixty kilometers) thick!

The deepest anyone has ever drilled is only around seven and a half miles (twelve kilometers). So you can forget about digging a hole to the center of the Earth. That hole would have to be 4,000 miles (6,370 kilometers) deep!

The crust under the oceans is thin, but it is made up of very dense, heavy rock, which forms when erupting lava cools very quickly. This rock, called **basalt,** makes up most of the Earth's crust.

The heat inside the Hatchery keeps our dragon eggs warm.

Volcanoes come from natural holes or cracks in the crust. In some areas, the hot rock of the mantle begins to melt. The melted rock is called **magma.** Deep under Earth's surface, magma pools form in pockets called **magma chambers.** Magma is lighter than the

Lava flow in Hawaii

solid rock around it, and this makes it float. Where there are cracks or weak spots in the crust, the magma keeps rising. If there is a crack in the surface, the melted rock escapes, and a volcano forms!

The hot, melted rock that erupts from a volcano is known as **lava.** If lava and ash keep escaping, a hill or mountain builds up. This can happen quickly, or it can take thousands of years.

Just how fast can a volcano form? Imagine this: In 1943, in central Mexico, a farmer was out plowing his field. Suddenly he heard a noise like thunder. He looked up, but there wasn't a cloud in the sky. He felt the ground begin to shake beneath his feet. A crack opened up in his field!

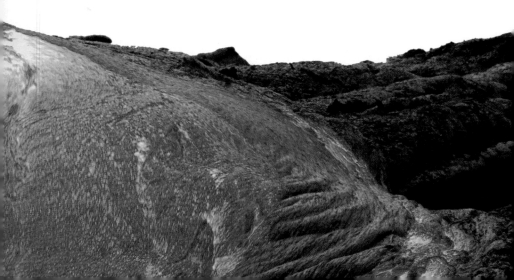

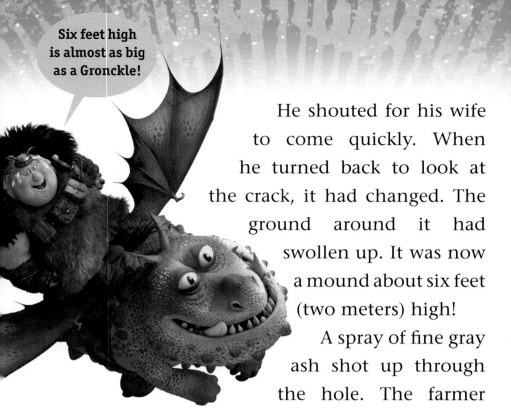

He shouted for his wife to come quickly. When he turned back to look at the crack, it had changed. The ground around it had swollen up. It was now a mound about six feet (two meters) high!

A spray of fine gray ash shot up through the hole. The farmer heard a loud hiss and noticed a smell like rotten eggs. The farmer and his family ran away from the farm. They were smart!

The explosions became more and more violent. By the end of the week, the mound had turned

Parícutin volcano in Mexico

into a volcanic cone. It was nearly 500 feet (150 meters) high! Two months later, it was twice as tall. The volcano was named Parícutin after a nearby village.

After about a year, Parícutin slowed down. For the next nine years, it only erupted once in a while, until it finally stopped. By then, the volcano was a small, 1,400-foot (424-meter) mountain!

The town of Parícutin was buried in lava and ash, but everyone got away safely.

Should you worry about a volcano erupting in your backyard? No! Volcanoes only appear where there are weak spots in Earth's crust.

Cathedral ruins in Parícutin

Here in Berk, we're ready for anything.

3

Where Do Volcanoes Form?

If you wanted to see a volcano for yourself, where could you find one? Many of Earth's volcanoes are around the Pacific Ocean. A long chain of volcanoes runs along the western coasts of North and South America, continuing all the way to the islands of Japan, Indonesia, and New Zealand. Altogether, there are more than 450 volcanoes in this chain! They form a huge circle around the ocean called the **Ring of Fire.**

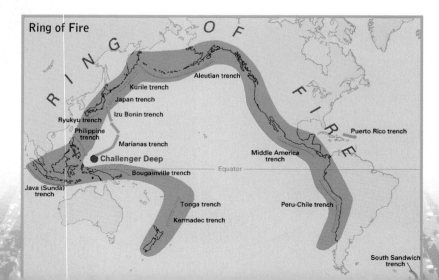

Ring of Fire

Aleutian trench
Kurile trench
Japan trench
Izu Bonin trench
Ryukyu trench
Philippine trench
Marianas trench
Challenger Deep
Bougainville trench
Java (Sunda) trench
Equator
Tonga trench
Kermadec trench
Middle America trench
Puerto Rico trench
Peru-Chile trench
South Sandwich trench

Why are there so many volcanoes in this area? To find out, geologists look at Earth's layers. The crust and top layer of the mantle together make up the **lithosphere.** Think of it as a hard shell around the Earth. But this shell isn't just one piece of solid rock—it's broken up into huge chunks known as **plates.** There are about a dozen major plates and several smaller ones—all of which are always moving! The layer of super-hot rock below them is soft and mushy. The plates drift very slowly, like rafts, over this softer layer of rock.

When scientists come to a conclusion based on their observations, it is known as a **theory.** The idea of plate movement is called the **theory of plate tectonics.**

When Vikings find a new dragon species, we get to name it! The names usually come from the characteristics of the dragon.

Volcanoes almost always happen at the edges of plates. In some places, plates are moving away from each other. In other areas, plates are slowly moving toward each other. In the Ring of Fire, most of the volcanoes form where plates are moving together. When a plate under the ocean moves toward a plate covered by land, the oceanic plate slowly sinks under the land, or continental, plate. This process is called **subduction,** and it happens because oceanic crust is heavier than continental crust.

As the oceanic plate slides down, water gets carried with it. The water makes the hot rock of the mantle melt fast and magma forms. At the same time, cracks open up in the continental crust. The magma rises through the weak spots. It keeps moving higher and higher until a volcano erupts!

All along the Ring of Fire, oceanic plates are sinking under continental plates. It's no wonder that three-quarters of all Earth's volcanoes are in the Ring of Fire. The edges of the oceanic crust

Subduction

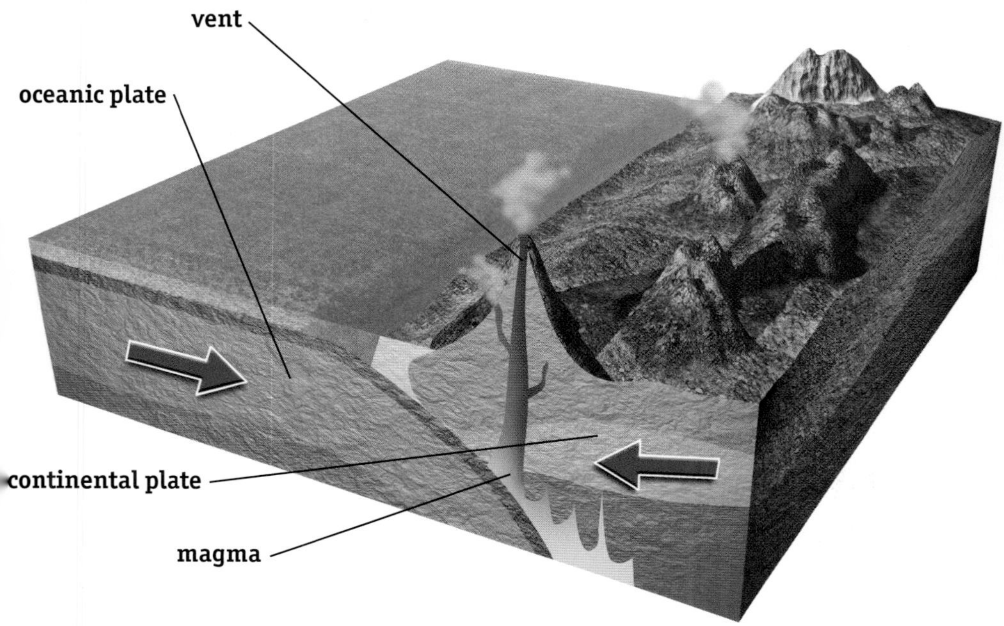

vent

oceanic plate

continental plate

magma

become part of the mantle, and volcanoes form as the continental crust crumples and cracks.

The volcanoes you've heard of are probably all on land. But volcanoes even erupt underwater! Most underwater volcanoes happen in areas where plates are moving apart. **Rifting** is the term used when plates separate. In rifting, long, deep cracks called **rifts** open up. Magma from the mantle rises, and lava spills out. The lava hardens and builds up on both sides of the rift. This lava becomes new oceanic crust.

Geologists have spent years studying the Ring of Fire, but they still have some volcano mysteries to solve. Sometimes a volcano erupts away from the edge of a plate, and geologists are not sure why. The volcanoes that make up the island chain of Hawaii are an example.

Kauai island in Hawaii

Berk has its own volcano.

The Hawaiian Islands are right in the middle of the Pacific Plate, and scientists think there may be a tall column of very hot rock, called a **mantle plume,** below them. These plumes are sometimes known as hot spots.

The oldest Hawaiian island likely formed over a plume about twenty-eight million years ago. The Pacific Plate is slowly moving toward the northwest. If the plume stayed in the same place, the first island would have been carried away in that direction. Eventually, another volcanic island would have formed over the plume. And then another and another. Because of the arrangement of Hawaii's islands, it looks like that's exactly what happened!

Today, eight major islands make up the state of Hawaii, along with almost 130 smaller islands. The island of Hawaii is the biggest and youngest of all. It was built up from five volcanoes. Another island, Loihi, is forming right now! The top of the island is still more than a half mile under the ocean's surface . . . but someday, it may rise high enough for people to live on!

Hawaii Volcanoes National Park

Different Types of Eruptions

In some ways, volcanoes are just like dragons: a little fiery, a little unpredictable . . . and no two look the same! If you want to learn more about the different types of volcanic eruptions, you should look at the kind of magma involved. Volcanoes have magma that's thick and sticky or thin and runny.

Where magma is thick, like in the Ring of Fire, volcanoes have violent eruptions. This is because the gloppy magma clogs up the volcanoes' vents. At first, the magma is

Tungurahua volcano in Ecuador

trapped underground, and pressure builds up. Then it breaks through the blocked-up vent. Super-hot water and gases bubble up and escape. Picture a bottle of soda. When you shake the bottle, bubbles fizz and pressure builds up. Quickly take off the cap and—*BOOM!* The soda explodes out of the opening!

When the volcano vent opens up, lava shoots out. The gases that escape make the sticky lava explode. The tiny pieces of lava are what make up **volcanic ash.** The ash goes flying into the air.

Anak Krakatau volcano in Indonesia

Volcanic ash can make a huge mess—and be very deadly. But even more dangerous things can come zooming out of volcanoes. Sometimes great blobs of lava fly up, cool off in flight, and get rounded in shape. Nearby rocks get broken up, too. Large chunks go flying. These blobs and chunks can be huge—sometimes as big as a house! Scientists have given them a very fitting name: **volcanic bombs**! And they are thrown through the air with *a lot* of force.

Once the explosion stops, the lava and rocks lose power. Everything falls back to Earth. But that's just the beginning! Hot ash, poisonous gases, and rock bombs tumble down the side of the volcano.

Pyroclastic f

They can fall as fast as 250 miles per hour (400 kilometers per hour). These volcanic avalanches are named **pyroclastic flows.** When one comes crashing down, nothing is safe. No living thing can escape its path of destruction!

Lava, ash, and chunks of rock pile up. Over the course of many eruptions, this buildup creates the most familiar shape for a volcano: a volcanic cone.

Volcanic cone of Ngauruhoe volcano in New Zealand

After an eruption is finished, any lava that hasn't shot out usually sinks back down into the vent and turns solid. That leaves a bowl-shaped **crater** at the top of the volcano.

A steep hill made of cooled lava—that definitely sounds like our Hatchery!

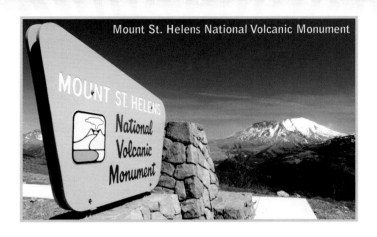

Mount St. Helens National Volcanic Monument

Mount St. Helens is a famous volcano in the Ring of Fire. In 1980, the whole northern side of the mountain began to bulge and crack. For many days, the bulge grew bigger and bigger. The magma under the mountain was rising. Then, one morning, an earthquake shook the area, and the bulge gave way. A huge wall of rock plunged down the mountain.

This released a lot of pressure from the magma chamber. The magma frothed up, and the top of the mountain exploded! Smoke and ash darkened the skies for miles around. A pyroclastic flow destroyed a big patch of forest below.

Sometimes the rocks and ash from an eruption mix with a lot of water. This creates a volcanic mudflow, known as a **lahar.** Lahars can cover vast areas in a thick, sticky layer of mud. Some lahars run deep and fast, and when that happens, watch out! They can quickly flatten villages, burying thousands of people.

In some hot spots, like Hawaii, eruptions are not explosive. They are gentler and last longer. This is because the magma is thin and runny. For example, Mauna Loa has been gently erupting over and over again for about a million years. Lava oozes from the volcano's vent, and streams of lava flow down the sides.

A Hawaiian volcano erupting lava into the Pacific Ocean

Mauna Kea summit overlooking Mauna Loa in the distance

Mauna Loa is a **shield volcano.** It is built up of thousands of layers of lava. This gives it a wider, flatter shape, which makes it look like a warrior's shield. Mauna Loa is the largest shield volcano on Earth. If you measure it from the seafloor to its top, it's taller than Mount Everest!

Shield volcanoes do not have pyroclastic flows. Instead, they have slower lava flows. The molten lava glows red hot, and as it cools, it gets thicker and gooier. When it has cooled completely, the lava turns hard and dark in color.

As lava flows down the side of a volcano, it takes on interesting shapes. These shapes are named after

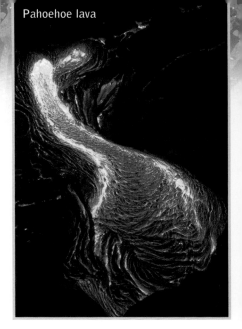
Pahoehoe lava

Hawaiian words. **Pahoehoe** (pah-HOE-eh-hoe-eh) forms from thin, fast-flowing lava. The lava spreads out in sheets. The surface layer cools, but under the surface, molten lava keeps moving. This twists and folds the thin surface layer into smooth, ropy shapes.

A'a (AH-ah) forms as lava cools and grows thicker. The surface layer gets a rough texture. Under the surface, lava keeps flowing, and the surface breaks into chunky blocks. Even if lava flows are slow, they can be very dangerous. A large lava flow can bury a whole town!

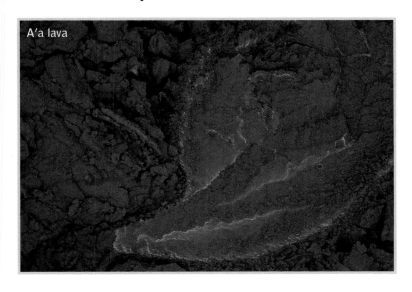
A'a lava

We now know that different volcanoes erupt in different ways. But sometimes even the same volcano changes its mind! Mount Fuji and Mount Vesuvius have both had explosive *and* gentle eruptions.

A volcano made from many layers of lava, rock, and ash is called a **stratovolcano.** *Strato* is a Latin word that means "layer."

Sometimes a "hot spot" can create another type of volcano: a **supervolcano.** Supervolcanoes are never gentle! In these areas, heat from the mantle melts a big area of crust. A lot of very sticky magma builds up in a huge shallow chamber. Thinner, runnier magma continues to pool even deeper below. The runnier magma rises in places, and gases bubble up. The pressure on the sticky magma chamber above grows and grows. When

Even dragons can be of two minds. Barf and Belch rarely agree with each other!

the pressure becomes too great, a massive eruption can occur!

One example of a supervolcano is the Yellowstone supervolcano. This supervolcano has erupted at least three times in the past. The last time was 640,000 years ago. Once a supervolcano erupts, it doesn't leave behind a cone. Instead, ash and rocks are shot out over thousands of square miles. The magma chamber sinks, leaving behind a wide, shallow hole called a **caldera.**

Yellowstone National Park in Wyoming

At the Ashfall Fossil Beds State Historical Park in Nebraska, you will see fossils of rhinos, camels, and other prehistoric beasts that were buried in ash. This happened when the Yellowstone hot spot erupted twelve million years ago. The red tags you see here are used by scientists for identification purposes.

The Yellowstone supervolcano has a caldera that is larger than the state of Rhode Island!

Supervolcanoes may be big, but they do not make the biggest volcanic eruptions. The largest ones are under the oceans, where plates are moving apart. The narrow undersea rifts can run for thousands of miles. The eruptions are usually slow and gentle, but they release tons of hot lava. When the lava hits the cold seawater, it cools quickly. This creates **mid-ocean ridges.** An example of this is the Mid-Atlantic Ridge, which has been building up for more than 200 million years.

World Distribution of Mid-Ocean Ridges

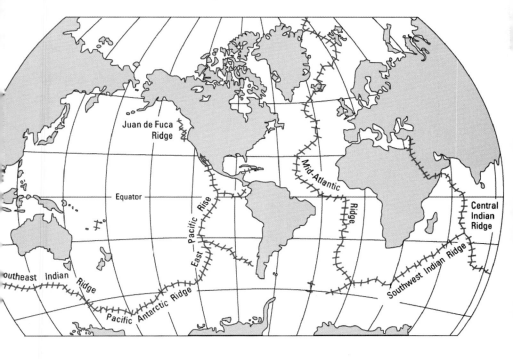

When Will It Erupt?

If you live next to a volcano, you probably want to know if or when it will erupt! The answer could be *very soon!* But it could also be *never.* Volcanoes can be **active, dormant,** or **extinct.** A dormant volcano is one that has not erupted for a very long time. Nearby towns are probably safe. An active volcano, on the other hand, is one that has

Mount Visoke in Africa

erupted within the past few hundred years, or is showing signs that it may erupt soon. Around the world, more than fifty volcanoes erupt each year.

Volcanoes become extinct when they are completely cut off from their source of magma. Extinct volcanoes are the only safe volcanoes. All active volcanoes can be dangerous. And even dormant volcanoes can quickly pose a threat. Do you remember Mount Vesuvius? Before it erupted in 79 CE, it had been quiet for eight hundred years. You never know when a sleeping volcano will wake up.

Berk's volcano hasn't rupted for a long time . . . but we should still be careful!

Mount Vesuvius towering over Naples in Italy

It might be hard to imagine that people would want to live near such a danger. But more than two million people live near Mount Vesuvius today. Because so many people live there, scientists consider it one of the most dangerous volcanoes on the planet! Vesuvius has erupted many times since 79 CE. It could erupt again at any time. That would mean big trouble for those who live nearby, as most of its eruptions have been explosive.

If you're going to live near an explosive mountain, you need smart, prepared people to help protect you. **Volcanologists** are geologists who study volcanoes. They keep a close watch over active volcanoes like Mount Vesuvius. Today, scientists know more about volcanoes and have better tools than they did in ancient times. They are better able to predict when a volcano might erupt.

What are some key signs that an eruption is about to take place? Tiny earthquakes are a very common clue. When it looks like an old volcano is becoming restless, volcanologists move in fast. They place seismometers all around the volcano. The seismometers can pick up very faint vibrations— even ones that might be too small for people to feel.

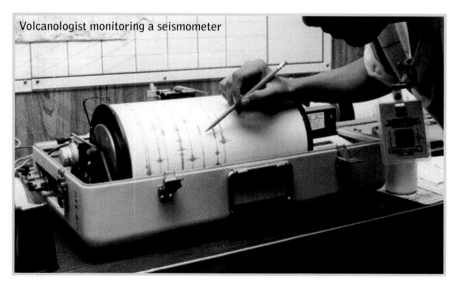

Volcanologist monitoring a seismometer

When magma begins to rise up through a volcano's vent, it makes the whole mountain shake. The seismometers record these vibrations, and volcanologists study them. These vibrations are like a code, and different patterns tell volcanologists what might be happening. Certain patterns usually happen before an eruption. When scientists start to see them, they go on high alert. There is no way to be sure *exactly* when a volcano will erupt, so they must study the mountain carefully, looking at every clue.

Volcanologists look at the rock and ash from old eruptions. Understanding a volcano's past helps them create **hazard maps.** Hazard maps show which areas around the mountain could

My dad, Stoick the Vast, is our fearless leader. It's his job to make big decisions. If the volcano erupts, Stoick will know what to do.

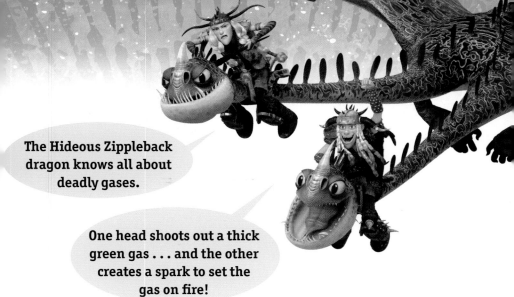

The Hideous Zippleback dragon knows all about deadly gases.

One head shoots out a thick green gas . . . and the other creates a spark to set the gas on fire!

be in the most danger. If the signs get worse, the people who live in these areas will be the first to move out.

If a volcano is about to erupt, it may also begin to give off steam or poisonous gases. These gases may come from the central vent or from smaller cracks in the volcano's sides.

Kawah Ijen volcano in Indonesia

Fumarole on Mutnovsky volcano in Russia

Small cracks in the side of a volcano are called **fumaroles.** Volcanologists watch these very carefully. They even use special detectors to keep track of the gas. Volcanologists look for even the tiniest of changes, as they could be a sign that something is about to happen. For example, what happens if the gas has a little more sulfur dioxide? For one thing, it will get very stinky! This chemical has a rotten-egg smell!

I love the smell of rotten eggs! Every Viking worth his or her salt has a little stench.

But more importantly, this would tell a volcanologist that magma is on the move.

Volcanologists also keep an eye on the shape of the mountain. If they see any bulges or cracks, they can tell that an eruption may be near. Volcanologists depend on modern technology for such an important job. From out in space, satellites help them watch for changes. Satellites can detect even the smallest crack or bulge!

Satellites can also warn volcanologists about changes in heat. As magma rises, the ground around a volcano often becomes warmer, and special satellites can pick up on changes in ground temperatures.

All these clues help volcanologists predict what a volcano might do next. If the signs look bad, they warn the local towns and help them prepare for disaster. People in these areas must have a plan in place for getting out fast.

A volcanologist's gear:

• **Protective suit:** Many volcanologists get dangerously close to lava flows. Along with heavy boots and thick gloves, a protective suit can keep scientists safe from the extreme heat.

• **Gas mask:** Tiny, sharp grains of volcanic ash can harm lungs. A gas mask keeps out these particles. It can also lower the risk of breathing in poisonous gases.

• **Thermometer:** Lava temperatures can be as high as 2,200 degrees Fahrenheit (1,200 degrees Celsius). Hot lava would melt an ordinary glass thermometer. Volcanologists use an electric thermometer made of metal.

• **A pen and notebook:** Of course!

A volcanologist ascends the rim of Mount Nyiragongo in the Democratic Republic of the Congo.

The United States Geological Survey (USGS) aids people in need. They have a Volcano Disaster Assistance Program (VDAP). If any country is worried about a particular volcano, VDAP's team of volcanologists is ready to go. They help local scientists figure out if the volcano will erupt soon and how big that eruption might be. This gives people the information they need to decide if and when to leave the area.

VDAP experts are always working to make better tools to observe volcanoes. They also train scientists in many areas around the world.

A USGS scientist monitors a Global Positioning Station on Mount St. He

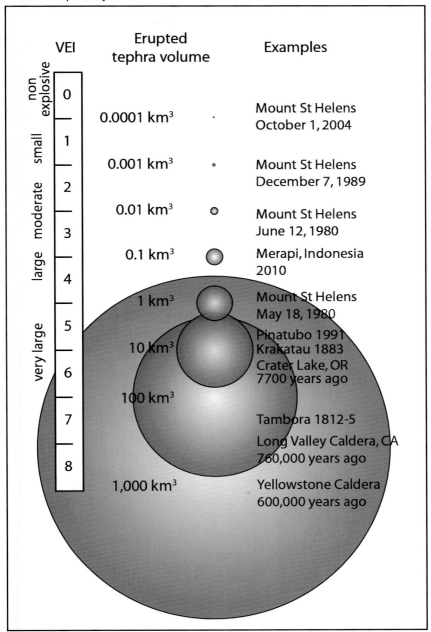

Volcanoes Rock!

Volcanoes can be scary and dangerous. But they can do plenty of good, too! As soon as hot molten lava comes out of a volcano, it begins to cool. It gets thicker and harder. When the lava hardens completely, it becomes brand-new rock!

The rocks on Berk were used to build the training grounds and School of Dragons lab!

Rocks are just about everywhere you look. People use them in many different ways. A **rock** is a solid material made up of one or more minerals. **Minerals** are substances that are formed in nature.

Each mineral has its own color and hardness, and its own special structure or shape. Geologists call this shape the mineral's **crystal** structure.

There are three types of rock: **igneous, sedimentary,** and **metamorphic.** The rocks on Earth are always changing (sometimes very slowly). This process is known as the **rock cycle.** Volcanoes have an important part to play in this process.

Amethyst

Rock that forms when lava or magma cools is igneous rock. Even though **igneous** rocks may come from the same super-hot liquid, they can look and feel very different. This is because of how slowly or quickly they cool. When lava cools quickly, the crystals in the rock are small. Sometimes they are so small that they are hard to see. This gives the rock a smooth texture.

Obsidian (volcanic glass)

What about when the magma cools slowly underground? This allows the rock's crystals time to grow bigger, which gives the rock a rougher texture. It's easy to see and feel the crystals in these rocks. **Granite** is an example of igneous rock that has cooled slowly. This strong rock may be easy to recognize since it's used in many buildings.

Pink granite

Types of Igneous Rocks

Igneous comes from the Latin word ignis, which means "fire."

Basalt is made up of quartz and feldspar that cooled quickly.

Granite is made up of crystals of quartz, feldspar, and biotite that cooled slowly underground.

Rhyolite is made up of crystals of quartz, feldspar, and biotite that cooled quickly aboveground.

Gabbro is made up of crystals of pyroxene, olivine, and feldspar that cooled slowly underground.

Gabbro

Volcanoes make new igneous rock. But almost as soon as new rock forms, it begins to break down. Over time, this forms **sedimentary** rock. First, the forces of weather slowly grind the rock into tiny grains of **sediment.** Giant rocks might not be so easy to move, but tiny bits of sediment are moveable. Flowing water sweeps up sediment and carries it away. Eventually, the stream of water slows down. Then the sediment sinks and settles, and layers of it build up.

All those layers of sediment press down on top of each other. The grains of sediment get squeezed closer together. As the water dries up, it leaves minerals behind. These minerals bond the grains together. They have made a brand-new kind of rock from tiny pieces of older ones!

Sedimentary rock cliffs

Sand and mud are two kinds of sediment. Grains of sand are bonded together to form **sandstone.** Mud turns into **mudstone.**

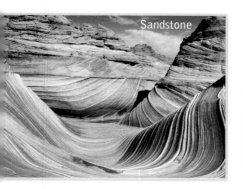
Sandstone

Mudstone

As sediment layers form on top of each other, they can bury some amazing secrets . . . like fossil bones! After a bone gets stuck in a layer of sediment, minerals fill in all its tiny pores. This can **preserve,** or save, the bones for hundreds of millions of years.

prehistoric fish fossil in sedimentary rock

Sometimes we find fossil bones when we go exploring!

The third kind of rock, **metamorphic** rock, is made from heat and pressure deep inside the Earth. Sometimes it is formed by the heat of a volcano. Igneous rock is created from cooling magma or lava. But under the surface, any rock that is near the rising magma gets heated like bread dough in an oven. The baking process changes the rock.

Marble is a type of metamorphic rock formed when limestone is squeezed and folded.

Metamorphic rock can also form where tectonic plates collide. One plate slides under the other, and great pressure and heat build up. The rock here is squeezed, stretched, and folded—and ultimately changed forever.

Tremendous heat and pressure slowly change the crystal structures of rock, turning them into new kinds of rock.

With heat and pressure, igneous and sedimentary rock can turn into metamorphic rock. Likewise, older metamorphic rock can change into different kinds of metamorphic rock. Check out the chart below and see if you can spot the differences!

 Granite turns into **gneiss.**

 Basalt turns into **schist.**

 Limestone turns into **marble.**

 Sandstone turns into **quartzite.**

 Slate turns into **phyllite.**

No wonder we have so much farming on Berk. The minerals in our soil help us hungry Vikings grow nutrient-rich food.

Volcanic ash is rock that has exploded. Like all rock, it is made up of minerals. When ash falls to the ground, minerals make the soil better for growing crops. That's one reason why many people live near volcanoes, in spite of the dangers.

All types of rocks are useful for people. We use them to build houses, schools, and libraries. We use rock to pave roads and sidewalks, and to create beautiful sculptures. The minerals in rocks give us the rich soil we need to grow our food. In these ways, volcanoes can be very useful!

7

Volcanoes in Space

If you could take a trip across the solar system, you'd notice something amazing. Earth is not the only place with volcanoes!

Look up at the full moon at night. Do you see the dark craters? Some say they look like the face of the "Man in the Moon." They are really huge fields of hardened lava.

The Moon

The first eruptions on the Moon happened between three and four billion years ago. Back then, the Moon was bombarded with giant meteorites. Every time a meteorite crashed into the Moon, the heat and force of impact cracked open its outer shell, and molten lava poured out.

Can you imagine the Moon covered in lines of fire-red lava? That sounds out of this world! You won't see any eruptions if you look up at the night sky these days. The Moon's last major volcanic eruptions were about one billion years ago.

A robotic spacecraft that orbits the Moon has sent back images of much smaller volcanoes that may have been erupting until as recently as 50 million years ago. But today, the Moon is probably too cool to erupt again, and collisions with meteorites are very rare.

If Earth and its moon have volcanoes, what about the other planets in our solar system?

View of Earth from the Moon

Venus

Venus has even more volcanoes than Earth does! But there is no Ring of Fire on Venus. Instead, its volcanoes have formed all over the surface. Unlike Earth, Venus does not have giant shifting plates. Venus has a thin crust, with many mantle plumes, or hot spots.

Space probes have also shown great fields of lava on Venus. They have seen groups of low "pancake domes" that have been pushed up by magma. And there are many wide calderas where domes have collapsed.

Some of Venus's volcanoes could still be active! Space probes have detected bright flashes near a giant shield volcano named Maat Mons. These could be signs of a fresh lava flow or an active hot spot.

Earth and Venus have some extra-large volcanoes, but the most gigantic volcano in the solar system is on Mars. It's known as Olympus Mons.

Olympus Mons on Mars

Olympus Mons has the shape of a shield volcano and spreads across an area as big as the state of Arizona. Its slopes are gentle, but it rises almost sixteen miles (twenty-five kilometers) above its base. That's like stacking three Mount Everests on top of one another!

Some of Mars's volcanoes, like Olympus Mons, formed from mantle plumes, or hot spots. Others, like Alba Mons, were probably caused by meteorites.

Alba Mons is one of the biggest lava fields in the solar system. Just how big is it? It's as wide as the entire United States! That's more than twenty times bigger than the largest lava flow on Earth.

All of Mars's volcanoes have been quiet for the past 500 million years. But scientists think some of them could become active again.

It wasn't until 1979 that humans first saw a volcano erupting in space. As the *Voyager 1* spacecraft flew past Jupiter, it sent back images of Io, one of the planet's larger moons. The images showed a big volcanic cloud. It looked like a giant

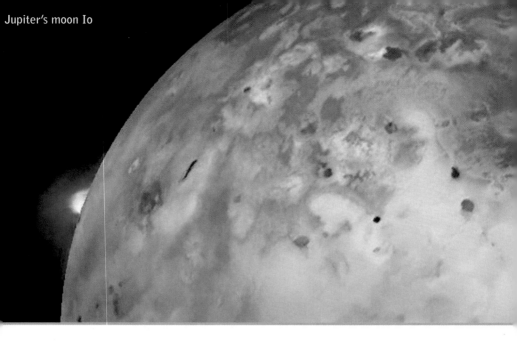

umbrella popping open into space! A little later, *Voyager 2* spotted several more volcanic clouds. Since then, scientists have counted more than one hundred active volcanoes on that moon alone!

More recently, scientists found something strange on Enceladus, one of Saturn's moons. They saw what looked like a huge geyser, shooting up hundreds of miles from the surface. On Earth, geysers erupt with scalding-hot water. But the upper layers of this moon are mostly made of ice! Could this weird geyser be a sign of volcanic activity? Yes! But there is no molten rock. Only water and gases erupt from volcanoes on ice worlds.

Ever wonder why
Saturn has rings?
Ice crystals and gases
from volcanoes
on Enceladus helped
create at least
one of them!

Saturn's moon Enceladus

rock core

ust of ice

water/ice mantle

Aren't volcanoes supposed to be hot? How can volcanoes erupt on ice worlds? The ice in the mantle of these worlds may get warmed in certain places. If cracks or weak spots appear in the icy crust, pressure is suddenly released. Water vapor and other gases shoot out. These are **cryovolcanoes.**

Other space probes have seen volcanoes erupting even farther out in space. There are volcanoes on one of Neptune's moons, Triton. That's billions of miles away from Earth! Triton's volcanoes are the most distant ones we've ever seen. But as we continue to explore the solar system and beyond, who knows what we may find? Perhaps there are different kinds of volcanoes erupting *everywhere* in the universe!

Glossary

a'a: A lava flow with a rough, rubbly surface.

active: Moving about or doing something. An active volcano is one that has erupted within the past few hundred years and is likely to erupt again.

basalt: A type of fine-grained igneous rock that can form when lava cools quickly.

caldera: A large volcanic crater. A caldera often forms after a volcano erupts, when the center of the volcano collapses into the empty magma chamber below.

crater: A steep, bowl-shaped hollow in the ground. A crater can form at the top of a volcano, or at the site where a large meteorite crashes into the surface of the Earth or another planet.

crust: The rock that makes up the outer layer of the Earth.

cryovolcano: An ice volcano. A cryovolcano erupts water and other gases rather than lava. There are no known cryovolcanoes on Earth.

crystal: A solid whose atoms are arranged in a particular shape, such as a cube or pyramid. Different minerals each have their own special crystal shape and color.

dormant: Resting, or inactive. A dormant volcano is one

that has not erupted for hundreds or thousands of years, but which may erupt again in the future.

extinct: No longer active. An extinct volcano is one that has erupted in the past but will not erupt again.

fumarole: A crack or hole in the Earth near a volcano, where volcanic gases leak out.

geologist: A scientist who studies rocks and minerals and the ways in which the Earth has changed over millions of years.

granite: A type of coarse-grained igneous rock that can form when magma cools slowly.

hazard map: A map of an area highlighting places where volcanic activity, such as lava flows and pyroclastic flows, have been most destructive in the past.

igneous rock: Rock that forms when hot molten lava or magma cools and becomes solid.

inner core: The hot, dense, ball-shaped center of the Earth. The inner core is made up mostly of iron and nickel.

lahar: A volcanic mudflow made up of volcanic rocks and ash mixed with water.

lava: Hot molten rock that has flowed out onto the Earth's surface.

lithosphere: The rigid outer layer of the Earth. The lithosphere is made up of the Earth's crust plus the upper layer of the mantle.

magma: Hot molten rock below the Earth's surface.

magma chamber: A space belowground filled with magma.

mantle: The thick layer of hot rock below Earth's crust and above the core.

metamorphic rock: A type of rock that forms when already-existing rock is changed by heat or pressure deep within the Earth.

mid-ocean ridge: An undersea mountain chain that forms where two oceanic plates are moving apart.

mineral: A solid substance found in the ground that does not come from living things. Each type of mineral has its own chemical makeup and crystal form.

mudstone: A blocky, fine-grained sedimentary rock formed when tiny particles of mud are pressed together and bonded, or cemented.

naturalist: A scientist who studies the plants, animals, minerals, and other things found in nature.

outer core: The layer of Earth's core that surrounds the inner core. The outer core is made up of hot liquid metal, mostly iron and nickel.

pahoehoe: A lava flow that has a smooth, ropy surface. It forms from thin, fast-flowing lava.

plate: One of the huge blocks, many miles thick and hundreds or thousands of miles wide and long, that make up the Earth's lithosphere.

Plinian eruption: Any huge volcanic eruption that is similar to the eruption of Vesuvius in 79 CE. The name honors Pliny the Younger, who wrote an accurate description of the eruption.

plume: A tall column of very hot rock that rises up from deep within the mantle. These are also sometimes referred to as hot spots.

preserve: To save something or make it last a long time. The remains of living things are sometimes preserved in sedimentary rock as fossils.

pumice: A light igneous rock that forms from frothy, or bubbly, lava.

pyroclastic flow: A fast-moving avalanche of hot volcanic rock, dust, and ash mixed with air that rolls down the side of an erupting volcano.

rift: A very long, deep crack that appears in the Earth's crust where two plates are moving apart.

rifting: In plate tectonics, the process of two plates moving apart.

Ring of Fire: A nickname for the long, nearly circular arrangement of active volcanoes that occur around the edge of the Pacific Plate.

rock: A naturally occurring solid, made up of one or more minerals.

rock cycle: The set of natural processes that change rocks of each of the three types—igneous, sedimentary, and metamorphic—into the other two types.

sandstone: A coarse-grained sedimentary rock formed when grains of sand are pressed together and bonded, or cemented.

sediment: A collection of loose mineral grains, such as sand, mud, or pebbles, which are not bonded, or cemented, together.

sedimentary rock: Any rock that forms when sand, mud, pebbles, or other pieces broken off from already-existing rocks are pressed and bonded, or cemented, together.

seismometer: A tool that can measure the shaking of the Earth that happens during an earthquake or volcanic eruption.

shield volcano: A volcano with a broad, gentle dome.

stratovolcano: A large, cone-shaped volcano with alternating layers of lava and material from pyroclastic flows.

subduction: The process through which one tectonic plate sinks down and pushes under another plate.

supervolcano: An immense volcano that shoots out more than 240 cubic miles (1,000 cubic kilometers) of lava, dust, and ash in one eruption. No supervolcanoes have erupted in recorded human history.

theory: An explanation based on experiments and observations of how or why something happens. Theories help predict future events and are supported by a great deal of evidence.

theory of plate tectonics: The idea that the outer layer of the Earth, the lithosphere, is made up of several separate plates that move slowly over the mantle.

Vesuvius: An active volcano near Naples, Italy.

volcano: An opening or vent in Earth's crust through which lava, ash, and hot gases flow during an eruption. A volcano can be described as active, dormant, or extinct.

volcanic ash: Tiny bits and pieces of minerals and glass that form when hot lava explodes and cools quickly in the air.

volcanic bomb: A large chunk of rock or blob of sticky lava thrown into the air during a volcanic eruption.

volcanic cone: A shape that many volcanoes form when lava, ash, and chunks of rock pile up over time.

volcanologist: A geologist who studies volcanoes.

INDEX